T0087405

PACIFIC COAST HORNS

LONGHORN
SERENADE

TROMBONE

MUSIC MINUS ONE

3975

SUGGESTIONS FOR USING THIS MMO EDITION

We have tried to create a product that will provide you an easy way to learn and perform these compositions with a full ensemble in the comfort of your own home. The following MMO features and techniques will help you maximize the effectiveness of the MMO practice and performance system:

Because it involves a fixed accompaniment performance, there is an inherent lack of flexibility in tempo. We have observed generally accepted tempi, and always in the originally intended key, but some may wish to perform at a different tempo, or to slow down or speed up the accompaniment for practice purposes; or to alter the piece to a more comfortable key. For maximum flexibility, you can purchase from MMO specialized CD players & recorders which allow variable speed while maintaining proper pitch, and vice versa. This is an indispensable tool for the serious musician and you may wish to look into purchasing this useful piece of equipment for full enjoyment of all your MMO editions.

We want to provide you with the most useful practice and performance accompaniments possible. If you have any suggestions for improving the MMO system, please feel free to contact us. You can reach us by e-mail at *info@musicminusone.com.*

3975

CONTENTS

ISBN 1-59615-785-2

Trombone

Bugler's Holiday

LEROY ANDERSON
arr. by P. CHAUVIN

The Barber of Seville Overture

Trombone

Gioacchino Rossini
Arr. by Charles Warren

8

In the Dark

Trombone

Bix Beiderbecke
Arr. by Charles Warren

Big Band Montage II

Trombone

Woodchopper's Ball, Cherry Pink and Appleblossom White,
Begin the Beguine, Opus One, Dream

arr. by P. CHAUVIN

3 taps- 1 1/2 measures

V. S.

MMO 3975

3 taps - 3/4 measure

12

Opus One
written by Sy Oliver

MMO 3975

I Wanna Be Like You

Trombone

Words and Music by
Richard M. Sherman and Robert B. Sherman

Trombone

Operatic Rag

Julius Lenzberg - Charles Warren

Take Five

Trombone

Paul Desmond
arr. by P. CHAUVIN

Flower Duet
From "Lakme"

Trombone

Leo Delibes
Arr. by Charles Warren

MMO 3975

When the Saints Go Marching In

Trombone

Traditional

MUSIC MINUS ONE
50 Executive Boulevard
Elmsford, New York 10523-1325
1.800.669.7464 (U.S.)/914.592.1188 (International)

www.musicminusone.com
e-mail: mmogroup@musicminusone.com